READING

by **Anne Marie Mueser**
John Alan Mueser

Project Editor: Sandra Kelley

Text: Design and Production by Harry Chester Associates

Illustrated by John W. Frost
Leonard B. Cole

THINGS TO REMEMBER ABOUT READING

Use these skills as you read.

DETAILS
Find and remember the important details.

SEQUENCE
Understand and remember the order in which things happens.

CONTEXT
To help you find the meaning of a word, use the words and sentences nearby.

MAIN IDEA
Put the details together and find the main idea.

INFERENCE
Find the meanings that are not stated, and draw conclusions.

CAUSE AND EFFECT
Understand what makes things happen and why.

PREDICTING OUTCOMES
Based on what you have read, tell what will happen next.

UNDERSTANDING CHARACTER
Find out about people through their words and actions.

Published by McGraw-Hill Learning Materials, 1997

DIRECTIONS

Do each step with a number. If you are working on speed of reading, do the steps with ★ too.

1. Find the right page.

★ Get a watch or timer. Start timing as soon as you begin to read.

2. Read the selection carefully. Be sure to read all of it.

3. Read the first item after the selection. Look at all the choices and then pick the best one. Mark your answer in the right space on your answer sheet.

	1	2	3	
1	a b c d	a b c d	a b c d	a
2	a b c d	a b c d	a b c d	a
3	a b c d	a b c d	a b c d	a

4. Do the rest of the items the same way you did the first one. Be sure to read all the choices before you pick and mark one.

★ Check your watch and stop timing. Write down the time it took you to complete the page.

5. Check your answers with the Answer Key. Write the number you got correct at the bottom of the page.

Answer Key

6. Mark the number you got right in the correct place on your Progress Plotter.

Progress Plotter

★ Mark your time in minutes on the Progress Plotter.

7. Find the correct place on the Skills Tracker for the page you have just finished. Circle the item number for any one you got wrong.

Skills Tracker

	1	2
Details	4	1, 2
Sequence	4	—
Context	2	4
Main Idea	1	—
Inference	3, 5, 6	3, 6
Cause & Effect	3	2
Pred. Outcomes	6	5
Underst. Char.	6	5, 6

8. If you got any items wrong, go back and try them again. Make sure you know how to do them.

Copyright © 1984, 1978 by SRA/McGraw-Hill. All rights reserved. Printed in the United States of America.

San Francisco is a beautiful city next to the water. The city has many steep hills. Ron and Sue Jacobs have a big house high on one of these hills. It overlooks the water. When they're not working, Ron and Sue like to go sailing.

One fine spring day, Ron and Sue were getting ready to try their brand-new sailboat. They were on their way to the water. The boat was on a trailer <u>attached</u> to the back of their pick-up truck. Sue was driving the truck, while Ron watched the boat out the rear window.

Suddenly the trailer broke loose from the truck. It went backwards down the hill on its own. Then it slammed right into the side of a parked car. The next thing Ron and Sue knew, their brand-new boat wasn't on the trailer anymore. The sailboat, all 2,000 pounds of it, had slid off the trailer onto the top of a parked automobile. There it sat—a sailboat on top of a car by the side of the road. What a sight!

1. This story is mainly about
    (a) living in San Francisco.
    (b) an odd event.
    (c) sailing a boat.
    (d) buying a boat trailer.

2. In this story, <u>attached</u> means
    (a) under.
    (b) hooked up to.
    (c) in love with.
    (d) cut loose from.

3. The boat was on the car because
    (a) it was too heavy.
    (b) no one wanted it.
    (c) it flew off Sue's car.
    (d) it slid off the trailer.

4. Before the trailer broke loose,
    (a) it was hooked to a truck.
    (b) it slid down the hill.
    (c) the boat went on a car.
    (d) Ron and Sue sailed the boat.

5. Things might have been different if
    (a) the trailer had been bigger.
    (b) Ron had stayed home.
    (c) they hadn't been on a hill.
    (d) Ron were driving.

6. You can be sure that Ron and Sue
    (a) won't ever sail again.
    (b) took time to reach the water.
    (c) went to buy two new boats.
    (d) will stop driving trucks.

Time _____ # Correct _____

2

Have you ever eaten horse meat? Or did you think that it was used just for dog food? In many states, horse meat can't be sold for people to eat. In some states people can buy it to use for food.

One man ate horse meat for two years. He didn't even know it. He thought the meat was beef. His wife and nine children knew it wasn't beef. But they didn't tell him that the steaks, chops, and hamburgers were meat from a horse.

Why did the man's family do that to him? Horse meat was much <u>cheaper</u> than beef. They thought he wouldn't eat the meat if he knew it was from a horse. So they didn't tell him.

The man seemed happy to eat the meat. It tasted good to him when he was hungry. Then one day he found out that the meat was not beef. How do you think he felt about being tricked like that? How would you feel?

1. The family in this story eats
    (a) what horses eat.
    (b) canned food.
    (c) horse meat.
    (d) dog food.

2. The man's wife bought horse meat because
    (a) her husband wanted it.
    (b) it cost less than beef.
    (c) she didn't like horses.
    (d) her children liked it.

3. The story hints that horse meat and beef
    (a) are both bad for you.
    (b) are best served hot.
    (c) cost nearly the same.
    (d) are much alike in taste.

4. Something <u>cheaper</u>
    (a) makes more noise.
    (b) tastes as good.
    (c) costs the same.
    (d) costs less.

5. When the man found out, he
    (a) never ate again.
    (b) probably was upset.
    (c) enjoyed his dinner.
    (d) bought some flowers.

6. The man didn't know he was eating horse meat because
    (a) he ate too fast.
    (b) no one told him.
    (c) he was not smart.
    (d) the kitchen was dark.

Time _____ # Correct _____

Pam and Dan Pisner love children, but for many years they didn't have any of their own. Then they happily told their friends they were <u>expecting</u> a baby. At last they were going to have a child of their own. Mrs. Pisner thought she might be having twins. She and her husband planned what they would do to take care of two babies.

Dan Pisner had been laid off from his job, and he hadn't found another one. Pam had a very good job, so she worked as long as she could before giving birth. The Pisners knew they would manage somehow.

Finally it was time for Mrs. Pisner to go to the hospital. Her husband went with her. Imagine their excitement and joy when they had not one, not two, but five babies! There were four boys and one girl.

The Pisners decided that Pam would go back to work in her office as soon as she was able to. Dan would stay home to take care of the babies. With five little ones to care for, he probably won't get out to job hunt for quite some time.

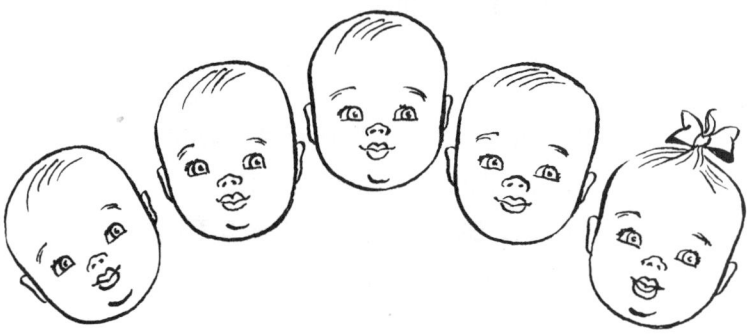

1. First, the Pisners were
    (a) going to the hospital.
    (b) having twins.
    (c) expecting a baby.
    (d) without any children.

2. <u>Expecting</u> means
    (a) understanding.
    (b) waiting for.
    (c) seeing well.
    (d) reaching out.

3. The Pisners were
    (a) worried about babies.
    (b) happy to be expecting.
    (c) working at two jobs.
    (d) training to be doctors.

4. Mr. Pisner will take care of the babies
    (a) while his wife works.
    (b) so Mrs. Pisner can rest.
    (c) because he's a doctor.
    (d) on most weekends.

5. The Pisners were joyful when
    (a) Dan lost his job.
    (b) Pam went back to work.
    (c) they had five babies.
    (d) they wanted a child.

6. The Pisner family is
    (a) very unhappy.
    (b) very wealthy.
    (c) like any other.
    (d) quite unusual.

Time _____ # Correct _____

4

Would you think a turtle could save a person's life? No? Well, one turtle did just that. This was not a pet turtle. It was too big to swim in a dish. You wouldn't want to keep it in the house. The turtle that saved the person's life was a giant sea turtle. It was more than three feet long!

One day the turtle was swimming in the Pacific Ocean. A big ship was going by. One of the sailors fell into the water. No one saw him fall, and the ship moved away. The man was alone in the water. He was sure he was going to die. Then he saw the turtle. He held on to the turtle's back. The two of them — man and turtle — swam along. At last help came. Many hours later, a <u>passing</u> ship saw the man and picked him up. The great turtle then swam away.

1. A sea turtle can't swim in a dish because
   (a) it likes salt water.
   (b) it's too big to fit.
   (c) sea turtles can't swim.
   (d) the dish would leak.

2. This story is mainly about
   (a) keeping a pet turtle.
   (b) large ships at sea.
   (c) falling off a ship.
   (d) how a turtle saved a life.

3. The sea turtle was
   (a) less than two feet long.
   (b) about four feet high.
   (c) more than three feet long.
   (d) smaller than most fish.

4. The ship went away because
   (a) it didn't like turtles.
   (b) the man was bad.
   (c) no one saw the man fall.
   (d) it was unable to stop.

5. In the story, <u>passing</u> means
   (a) going by.
   (b) just all right.
   (c) not failing.
   (d) racing.

6. It's likely that the man will
   (a) always fear turtles.
   (b) never forget the turtle.
   (c) stay at home.
   (d) swim again very soon.

Time _____ # Correct _____

5

Jennie Weston and Sunee Haws are young business women. They are both seven years old and in the second grade. What is their business? They sell jokes.

They call their company Sunee's Funnies for Jennie's Pennies. When their school, Hooper Elementary School, had a fair, they sold jokes for one cent each. They made $1.52 that day.

Someone told Johnny Carson, the <u>star</u> of television's "Tonight Show," about the girls and their jokes. Johnny invited them to appear on his show. The show paid them $200 to go on. At their usual rate of pay, they would have to tell 20,000 jokes to earn that much money.

Here's a sample of one of their jokes. Do you think it's worth a penny?

What do you get when you cross a giant with a skunk?

A big stink!

1. This story is mainly about
   (a) the Johnny Carson show.
   (b) a skunk and a giant.
   (c) two girls and jokes.
   (d) making money easily.

2. For each joke the girls
   (a) spend two days learning.
   (b) get $200.
   (c) get a penny.
   (d) make a lot.

3. The girls are named
   (a) Johnny and Penny.
   (b) Hooper and Carson.
   (c) Sunee and Jennie.
   (d) Pennie and Jennie.

4. Johnny Carson
   (a) went to Hooper School.
   (b) wrote jokes for the girls.
   (c) heard about the girls.
   (d) stopped telling jokes.

5. First the two girls
   (a) went on television.
   (b) sold jokes at a fair.
   (c) were paid $200.
   (d) met Johnny Carson.

6. The <u>star</u> of a show
   (a) has lots of lights.
   (b) is the top person.
   (c) works for no money.
   (d) makes one cent a joke.

Time _____ # Correct _____

6

What can happen to a baby who gets caught between a mother gorilla and a father gorilla? A baby gorilla at the Central Park Zoo in New York City found out the hard way.

Little Patty Cake stuck her arm out between the bars of her cage. Congo, her daddy, was in the next cage. Congo playfully grabbed the baby's little arm. Then Patty Cake's mother Lulu got upset. She pulled her baby away from the front of the cage. But, when Lulu pulled the baby, Congo still held on. Poor Patty Cake ended up with a broken arm.

Doctors took Patty Cake to the hospital. The little gorilla had to wear a cast on her arm for eight weeks. When she got better, she went back to live at the zoo again.

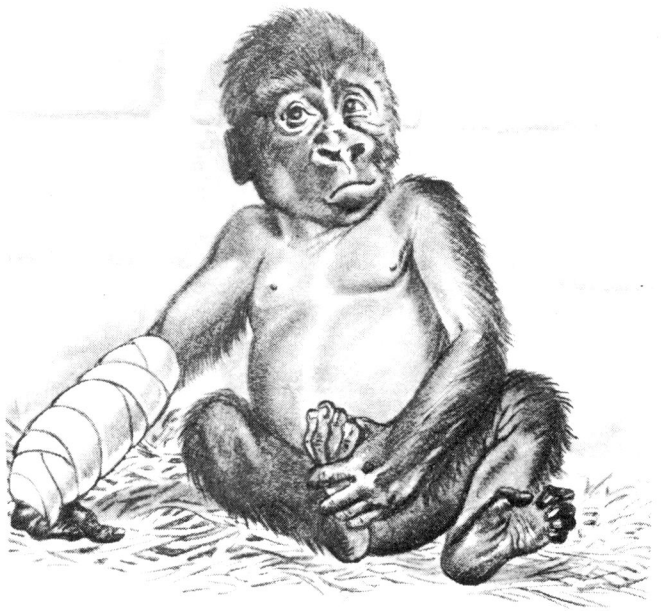

1. This story is mainly about
    (a) how Patty Cake got hurt.
    (b) playing gorilla games.
    (c) animals and their young.
    (d) Patty Cake's daddy.

2. Patty Cake and her father
    (a) didn't get along.
    (b) were both running wild.
    (c) lived with Lulu.
    (d) lived in separate cages.

3. The word playfully tells that
    (a) Congo likes bad games.
    (b) gorillas need playpens.
    (c) Congo didn't try to hurt.
    (d) Lulu was a good mother.

4. Patty Cake's mother
    (a) lived in another zoo.
    (b) enjoyed playing with her.
    (c) pulled her baby.
    (d) got out of her cage.

5. Patty Cake's arm broke because
    (a) it hit the cage door.
    (b) her parents pulled her.
    (c) she was on a bike.
    (d) someone hit her hard.

6. Which happened last? Patty Cake
    (a) went to the hospital.
    (b) broke her arm.
    (c) stuck her arm out.
    (d) had to wear a cast.

Time _____ # Correct _____

Tom Patterson is a science teacher who enjoys being outdoors. He likes going hiking. He likes walking through the woods and climbing mountains with a pack on his back. He used to prefer hiking alone. Chances are he won't be doing that anymore. Hiking alone can be dangerous.

One day Mr. Patterson was hiking in the Great Smoky Mountains. He wandered off the path. He stepped in a deep hole by mistake, and broke two bones in his left leg below the knee. He was in great pain, and with two broken bones he knew his hike was over.

After he broke his leg, Tom's biggest problem was that he was all alone out there in the mountains. He wasn't on the main trail, so there was a good chance that no one would come along and find him. Tom Patterson didn't want to die up there alone in the mountains. So he began to crawl.

He crawled through the bushes. He crawled across streams. He had to move very slowly because he hurt so much. He rolled his pack across the ground in front of him. He kept looking for a trail. He kept hoping that he would find someone to help him. Then another hiker, Bob Rezy, of Ohio, found him. "I just didn't want to die up there," said Patterson. In the four days he was crawling, he probably covered about a mile. That's not very far but it was far enough.

1. This story is mainly about
   (a) crawling instead of walking.
   (b) an injured hiker.
   (c) going to the mountains.
   (d) getting lost in trees.

2. Tom Patterson was a
   (a) math teacher.
   (b) swimming coach.
   (c) reading teacher.
   (d) science teacher.

3. Tom crawled because he
   (a) was tired of walking.
   (b) didn't like running.
   (c) was unable to walk.
   (d) lost his pack.

4. Which happened last?
   (a) Tom left the path.
   (b) A hiker found Tom.
   (c) Tom crawled a mile.
   (d) Tom broke his leg.

5. Tom stopped hiking because he
   (a) needed to rest.
   (b) reached his goal.
   (c) broke his leg.
   (d) needed to eat lunch.

6. When two people hike,
   (a) they often fight.
   (b) one could go for help.
   (c) all the food is used.
   (d) no one will get hurt.

Time _____ # Correct _____

8

Some people think dandelions are useful plants. Other people think they are weeds. Many people don't want dandelions to grow on their lawns. They want neat green grass without flowers and leaves in it. These people work hard to pull dandelions out of their lawns. Some even try to get rid of dandelions with weed killer.

It's pretty hard to kill dandelions. They are very strong plants. Some of the leaves stay green in winter even if the weather gets quite cold. Dandelions begin to <u>bloom</u> in the early spring. As soon as warm weather comes, they begin to have bright yellow flowers. The flowers close up tight at night. When the sun shines, they open up again.

Dandelion plants can be quite useful. The leaves can be eaten in salad. They also can be cooked and eaten as greens. Some people even make dandelion wine.

Is the dandelion a weed? What would you say if someone asked you that question?

1. Dandelions are
    (a) small pink flowers.
    (b) well-liked plants.
    (c) the worst weeds.
    (d) flowers or weeds.

2. Dandelion flowers open
    (a) any time it rains.
    (b) during the winter.
    (c) when the sun shines.
    (d) in a green salad.

3. To <u>bloom</u> is to
    (a) need cooking.
    (b) have flowers.
    (c) grow very large.
    (d) make salad.

4. Dandelions don't die in winter because
    (a) people pick them.
    (b) it doesn't get cold.
    (c) they are strong plants.
    (d) they close up at night.

5. People who call dandelions weeds
    (a) don't like them.
    (b) are always right.
    (c) don't drink wine.
    (d) use yellow flowers.

6. People who use dandelions
    (a) don't think they are weeds.
    (b) have very small lawns.
    (c) use lots of weed killer.
    (d) enjoy cold winters.

Time _____ # Correct _____

David Michaelowsky is a figure skater. That means he skates in a special way on the ice. Figure skating is a bit like dancing on the ice. It is not easy to do.

Good figure skaters have to work hard. They spend many hours skating, turning, twisting, and jumping. They practice so they can do well.

Like most figure skaters, David works hard. There is one big difference. David is deaf. He can't hear the music that plays while he skates. Even so, he does the figures on the ice in time to the music. How can he skate in time to the music when he can't hear it?

When he skates, David has a teacher, or coach, who helps him. His coach tells him when to start and when to stop, when to speed up and when to slow down. He uses hand signals to talk to David.

David skates very well. The people watching him clap hard and cheer him on. He can't hear them, but he can see their smiles. He is glad that they like to see him skate.

1. This story is mainly about
    (a) a deaf figure skater.
    (b) how to skate to music.
    (c) working on the ice.
    (d) how to go skiing.

2. Good figure skating takes
    (a) no time at all.
    (b) lots of hard work.
    (c) very loud music.
    (d) a coach with skates.

3. David isn't like other skaters
    (a) in the way he skates.
    (b) because he cannot hear.
    (c) because he falls more.
    (d) until he uses skis.

4. Figure skating is
    (a) done on the grass.
    (b) done to music.
    (c) easy to do.
    (d) nicest in summer.

5. To practice means to
    (a) watch someone else.
    (b) go to the movies.
    (c) listen to music.
    (d) work hard at something.

6. A deaf person
    (a) can't see.
    (b) talks a lot.
    (c) is too fat.
    (d) can't hear.

Time _____ # Correct _____

10

Tiger was glad to be home at last. She hadn't seen her family in a long time. She hadn't been home since summer vacation in Wisconsin, eight months earlier. Although it was snowy and cold at home in Iowa, Tiger seemed happy to be there again.

There was so much to tell about her 250-mile journey home, but Tiger did not speak. Her family had lots of questions, but Tiger wasn't giving any answers. Tiger is a cat.

Tiger's family didn't mean to leave her behind. They all had a happy vacation together. But nobody could find the cat when the car was packed and ready to go. Where had she been?

How had Tiger stayed alive for eight months away from home? How had she found her way home over so many miles? How had she crossed the Mississippi River? No one knows. Tiger got home healthy and fat. She just isn't telling anybody how she did it.

1. Tiger vanished
    (a) from a car in Iowa.
    (b) at the end of vacation.
    (c) to swim in the Mississippi.
    (d) for nearly eight years.

2. This story is about a cat that
    (a) always stays home.
    (b) enjoys catching mice.
    (c) was gone a long time.
    (d) doesn't like its home.

3. Tiger's home is in
    (a) Iowa.
    (b) Mississippi.
    (c) a pick-up truck.
    (d) Wisconsin.

4. Which happened last?
    (a) Tiger came home.
    (b) Tiger crossed the river.
    (c) The snow fell.
    (d) The vacation ended.

5. No one knows how Tiger got home
    (a) and no one really cares.
    (b) because cats can't tell.
    (c) because she crossed a river.
    (d) but it must have been easy.

6. A journey is a
    (a) travel story.
    (b) type of wagon.
    (c) short walk.
    (d) very long trip.

Time _____ # Correct _____

Have you ever seen an animal with three tails? This may sound like an odd question, but it really can be answered "yes."

There is a lizard called a gecko that sometimes has as many as three tails. Most of the time a gecko has only one tail, but it's possible for it to have three at one time. Here's how that happens.

If a gecko loses its tail, the tail grows back. If the tail only breaks a little bit, the gecko sometimes grows a new one anyway. Then there are two—the broken one and the new one. If a gecko breaks two tails a little bit, it can grow a third one. Then there are three.

Geckos live in warm countries. These lizards often live in trees, but many of them like people's houses best of all. Geckos can hold onto smooth surfaces such as walls and ceilings. People often <u>welcome</u> geckos because these lizards eat lots of insects. In some areas, people would rather have a few lizards in the house and not as many bugs.

A gecko would be an unusual and useful pet. But you should never try to catch a gecko by the tail. Can you figure out why?

1. This story is mainly about
    (a) an unusual lizard.
    (b) pets with too many tails.
    (c) a very strange insect.
    (d) how to kill insects.

2. To catch a gecko, you should
    (a) pull its feathers.
    (b) grab its tail.
    (c) reach for its body.
    (d) count its legs.

3. Geckos live in
    (a) cold countries.
    (b) evergreen forests.
    (c) large barnyards.
    (d) warm countries.

4. To <u>welcome</u> something is to
    (a) say goodbye to it.
    (b) feed it too much.
    (c) be glad to see it.
    (d) travel with it.

5. The best meal for a gecko would be
    (a) bird seed.
    (b) milk and cookies.
    (c) meat and vegetables.
    (d) insects.

6. If geckos did not eat bugs,
    (a) they would need sandwiches.
    (b) people might like them less.
    (c) they would need no food.
    (d) they would make good pets.

Time _____ # Correct _____

12

Do you like to eat fish? Have you ever tried catching one yourself? Fishing can be lots of fun. And people who fish often tell stories about the big fish that got away. The stories are often bigger than the fish.

Although he's only three years old, Michael Hoerr is very good at catching fish. One summer day, Michael and his parents went fishing at Swarthwood Lake, New Jersey. This lake has nice fresh water and quite a few fish.

Before the day was over, young Michael had caught the biggest fish of all. His prize catch was a large-mouth bass which was 22 inches long. It weighed 5 pounds 6 ounces. Michael had to use both arms to hold the fish so people could take pictures of it. Michael enjoyed holding his big fish for the <u>photographers</u>.

Michael explained that using the right kind of bait helped him catch his fish. He used worms—big juicy ones—as <u>bait</u>. When Michael gets older, he'll probably still be talking about his fish. This was one big one that didn't get away!

1. People who fish
   (a) always catch big ones.
   (b) often tell stories.
   (c) must take pictures.
   (d) like to dig worms.

2. Unlike most fishermen, Michael
   (a) uses worms for bait.
   (b) is only three years old.
   (c) never tells stories.
   (d) likes to catch bass.

3. <u>Bait</u> is used
   (a) to keep fish cold.
   (b) for lunch meat.
   (c) to make fish bite.
   (d) instead of a pail.

4. Michael used both arms to hold his fish because
   (a) the fish was so big.
   (b) he wanted to hug it.
   (c) his mother told him to.
   (d) the fish was jumpy.

5. <u>Photographers</u> are people who
   (a) like to go fishing.
   (b) eat large fish.
   (c) paint or draw.
   (d) take pictures.

6. To catch fish, Michael uses
   (a) a camera.
   (b) worms as bait.
   (c) his mother's boat.
   (d) hooks and bugs.

Time _____ # Correct _____

Harriet Ross was born on a large farm in Maryland in 1820. She was a slave. Her owner sent her to different places to work. She was treated badly. When she couldn't stand it any more, she ran away. She spent five days hiding in a pigpen. She had to fight the pigs for bits of food to eat. Harriet was tough. She knew how to stay alive.

Someone found Harriet, and she was beaten and sent home. From that time on, she worked outdoors. She learned to split rails and chop wood. She learned much about the outdoors from her father. He taught her how to walk quietly in the woods. He taught her which plants were good for food and which ones could help ease pain or cure illness. Harriet learned to find the North Star in the sky. All these things Harriet learned were helpful in her later life.

Years later, Harriet Ross, using the name Harriet Tubman, led many people north to be free. They hid in the woods. What Harriet knew about plants helped keep them alive. They followed the North Star. They found freedom.

1. This story is mainly about
    (a) Harriet as a young girl.
    (b) seeing the North Star.
    (c) hiding in a pigpen.
    (d) eating plants to live.

2. Harriet ran away because
    (a) she was a naughty girl.
    (b) running away was fun.
    (c) someone told her to.
    (d) people were cruel to her.

3. A tough person is
    (a) always nasty.
    (b) strong.
    (c) bright.
    (d) silly.

4. This story tells you that
    (a) plants never make good food.
    (b) hiding in the woods is fun.
    (c) some plants can save your life.
    (d) slaves had an easy life.

5. Which came first?
    (a) Harriet hid in the pigpen.
    (b) Harriet ran away.
    (c) Harriet was found.
    (d) Harriet ate pig food.

6. Harriet and her people followed the North Star
    (a) because they liked stars.
    (b) because it was pretty.
    (c) to eat plants in the woods.
    (d) to find their way north.

Time _____ # Correct _____

14

Before Americans sent a human into space, they sent a chimpanzee named Ham. On January 31, 1961, Ham blasted off from Cape Canaveral in Florida. The chimp was sent as our first astronaut to make sure the trip would be safe for people. It wasn't until Ham returned safely to Earth that space leaders dared to risk sending a human astronaut, Alan Shepherd. Now sending a person into space is quite common. But in 1961 it was unusual and very daring.

Ham, the first space chimp, stopped working in the space program in 1963. He spent most of the next twenty years living with humans. He didn't have any chimp friends at all. Then he went to live at a zoo in North Carolina where he met other chimpanzees. None of them had ever been in space, but they were like him in most other ways. Ham made special friends with Maggie, a lady chimpanzee. Ham died suddenly in the spring of 1983. Maggie was with him when he died.

1. Ham was
    (a) a very fine sandwich.
    (b) our first chimp in space.
    (c) unfriendly to others.
    (d) found in a park.

2. Which came last? Ham
    (a) left the space program.
    (b) went to the zoo.
    (c) went into space.
    (d) met Maggie.

3. Someone daring is
    (a) very quiet.
    (b) stupid.
    (c) brave.
    (d) in love.

4. Ham went into space first
    (a) because he wanted to.
    (b) by mistake.
    (c) to draw maps of it.
    (d) to see if it was safe.

5. The first human astronaut was
    (a) Ham himself.
    (b) Alan Shepherd.
    (c) a lady named Maggie.
    (d) left unnamed.

6. Twenty years before Ham died,
    (a) space travel was unusual.
    (b) Ham found a girlfriend.
    (c) people went to the moon.
    (d) he got very sick.

Time _____ # Correct _____

Alice and John Cannon, both in their 80s, were driving through Utah. They decided to take a little side trip through Dixie National Forest. That was a mistake. On April 15, 1983, their car got stuck in the mud on a lonely road. They couldn't move it at all. There was no one around to help.

The Cannons spent two nights in their car. When no one found them, they tried to walk out of the forest. This was hard, because Mr. Cannon's legs weren't strong. They went as far as they could. The next night they took some branches and bushes to cover themselves. The weather turned very cold and Mr. Cannon died in his sleep.

The next morning Mrs. Cannon began walking again. She found a cabin that was all locked up. The owners only used it in the summer. She broke in and found some cans of food. She found enough to eat to keep herself alive.

Mrs. Cannon was sure she would die in the cabin. She thought that no one would find her there until it was too late. She wrote a note to the people who owned the cabin. She told them she was sorry she had broken in. She said she hoped they would understand.

Mrs. Cannon's letter wasn't needed. Four days later the people looking for her found the cabin. They reached the woman in time to save her life.

1. This story is mainly about
    (a) life in the forest.
    (b) how a woman stayed alive.
    (c) bad roads in Utah.
    (d) walking near trees.

2. The Cannons' big mistake was
    (a) moving to Utah.
    (b) finding a cabin.
    (c) driving an old car.
    (d) taking a side road.

3. A lonely road
    (a) is always muddy.
    (b) has few people on it.
    (c) is very straight.
    (d) has ice and snow.

4. Mrs. Cannon wrote a note to
    (a) keep herself busy.
    (b) her family and friends.
    (c) say why she broke in.
    (d) the police who found her.

5. Which happened first?
    (a) John Cannon died.
    (b) The weather turned cold.
    (c) Mrs. Cannon kept walking.
    (d) The car stuck in the mud.

6. A cabin is a
    (a) large stone house.
    (b) small simple house.
    (c) place to keep a car.
    (d) shelf for canned food.

Time _____ # Correct _____

16

Heidi Musser was born <u>blind</u>. She didn't begin to talk or even make sounds like talking for a long time. Heidi's mother often sang to her baby and the child seemed to enjoy the music.

When Heidi was almost two years old, she was able to show that she did understand things. Even though she wasn't talking yet, Heidi listened well. One day, not too long before her second birthday, Heidi began to hum a song. It was a song her mother often sang to her. Heidi hummed it perfectly.

When Heidi first went to school, some people thought she was stupid. She wasn't stupid at all. She just couldn't see. When Heidi began taking piano lessons, people began to see just how smart she really was. Heidi did very well.

Heidi's piano teacher found that the child had an excellent ear. Even though Heidi couldn't read music, she listened to the pieces and remembered exactly the way each one should sound.

In 1983, at the age of 16, Heidi entered a contest to win a prize for piano playing. She was the only blind person to play there. She did beautifully. Heidi enjoyed playing for the people. Some day she may even teach music.

1. When Heidi was a baby,
    (a) she could see things.
    (b) talking came slowly.
    (c) her mother stayed away.
    (d) the school helped her.

2. Before Heidi talked, she
    (a) looked at things.
    (b) went to school.
    (c) ran away from home.
    (d) hummed a song.

3. This story is mainly about
    (a) learning the piano.
    (b) going to school.
    (c) singing and dancing.
    (d) a blind piano player.

4. A person who is <u>blind</u>
    (a) does not listen.
    (b) likes school.
    (c) cannot see.
    (d) must play music.

5. Heidi learned music by
    (a) listening to it.
    (b) reading the notes.
    (c) going to school.
    (d) helping her mother.

6. It's likely that Heidi will
    (a) give up the piano.
    (b) keep on with her music.
    (c) find a new teacher.
    (d) change to the drums.

Time _____ # Correct _____

In 1982, Britain and Argentina were at war in the Falkland Islands near South America. The war was short but fierce. It lasted 74 days. As in all wars, there were people killed and hurt.

It wasn't just humans that were killed. The soldiers killed many animals too, both those raised for food and many that were pets. Farmers in the Falklands asked the British to send animals to replace those lost in the war.

In the summer of 1983, the first ship full of animals left Britain for the Falklands. Much like Noah's Ark, this ship contained many different kinds of animals. There were 100 sheep from Wales and Scotland, and 29 sheepdogs to help the shepherds care for their flocks. There were ponies, horses, cows, goats, and pigs. The farmers were glad to receive so many fine animals. The children were happy that the ship carried ponies and pets.

1. The war in the Falklands
    (a) lasted a long time.
    (b) killed only animals.
    (c) was a good thing.
    (d) was short and fierce.

2. Flocks are
    (a) pieces of cloth.
    (b) barking dogs.
    (c) parts of a boat.
    (d) groups of sheep.

3. The British ship was like Noah's Ark because it
    (a) went in the rain.
    (b) was made of wood.
    (c) carried many animals.
    (d) had no small ponies.

4. The animals sent will provide
    (a) vegetables and fruit.
    (b) milk and meat.
    (c) entertainment.
    (d) chairs to sit on.

5. Shepherds are people who
    (a) fight in wars.
    (b) cook good meals.
    (c) raise small ponies.
    (d) take care of sheep.

6. This story suggests that
    (a) animals are bad.
    (b) wars are lots of fun.
    (c) war is not a good thing.
    (d) people are always cruel.

Time _____ # Correct _____

Did you ever lose something and wonder where it went? Somewhere there's a child who's probably wondering about a teddy bear. This teddy bear was left on an airplane in Australia. Its owner may never know that the bear has already traveled more miles than most people ever do.

No one could give the teddy bear back to the child who lost it because no one knew who that child was. So Teddy began <u>traveling</u> from place to place. He went everywhere by plane. Every time Teddy landed, the people who worked for the airline tried to find the bear's owner. When they didn't find the child, they put Teddy on the next plane.

Teddy kept going from one place to another looking for the child who had lost him. His brown fur became covered with airline tags. He even had a little book that listed the flights he had been on and the places he had been. If Teddy and his owner ever get together again, what a story the tags and book will tell.

1. This story is mainly about
    (a) airlines in Australia.
    (b) a boy named Teddy.
    (c) travels of a lost toy.
    (d) traveling with children.

2. A child on an airplane
    (a) became quite sick.
    (b) lost a live animal.
    (c) lost a teddy bear.
    (d) chewed on a blanket.

3. After several trips, Teddy had
    (a) a pain in his stomach.
    (b) tags on his fur.
    (c) a bad case of fleas.
    (d) a torn sweater.

4. <u>Traveling</u> means
    (a) getting lost.
    (b) going from place to place.
    (c) enjoying airplanes.
    (d) eating on a train.

5. No one sent Teddy home because
    (a) the airlines wanted him.
    (b) his owner didn't want him.
    (c) it would have cost a lot.
    (d) no one knew where home was.

6. If Teddy finds his owner, he probably will
    (a) get on the next plane.
    (b) stay home for a while.
    (c) scream very loudly.
    (d) eat a large lunch.

Time _____ # Correct _____

Can a person get in trouble for doing something good? That shouldn't happen, but once in a while it does. Here is a story about a woman who got in trouble for being nice to a lost dog.

Mrs. Rose saw a lost dog near her house. The dog looked hungry, so she gave it some food. A police officer saw her and asked if the dog was hers. She told him it wasn't. He didn't believe her and gave her two tickets. One was for having a dog off a leash. The other was because the dog had no tag on its collar.

Mrs. Rose was not happy. She didn't pay the tickets because she knew she was right. She went away for a few weeks to visit her grandchildren. She forgot all about the police officer and the tickets. The police tried to find her and make her pay. When she got back, she had to go to court.

The story does have a happy ending. Mrs. Rose went to court. When she told her story to the judge, he believed her. He said she should not have gotten the tickets. He didn't make her pay. The judge told her to keep being nice to animals.

1. Mrs. Rose seemed to be
   (a) a troublemaker.
   (b) unsure of herself.
   (c) a nice, kind person.
   (d) unusually forgetful.

2. Mrs. Rose fed the dog because
   (a) she wanted a new dog.
   (b) it was her animal.
   (c) the dog looked hungry.
   (d) the police told her to.

3. This story is mainly about
   (a) breaking the law.
   (b) feeding stray animals.
   (c) visiting grandchildren.
   (d) Mrs. Rose, a kind woman.

4. The police officer
   (a) did the right thing.
   (b) made a mistake.
   (c) disliked all dogs.
   (d) trusted Mrs. Rose.

5. The judge
   (a) did the right thing.
   (b) disliked all dogs.
   (c) made a mistake.
   (d) made Mrs. Rose pay.

6. Before anything else,
   (a) the police gave a ticket.
   (b) the judge helped Mrs. Rose.
   (c) the dog became lost.
   (d) Mrs. Rose got some food.

Time _____ # Correct _____

20

What color is an orange? Is it orange? Not always. Some oranges are green. They can be green in color even if they are <u>ripe</u> and ready to eat. An orange that is orange in color is one that has been grown in cool air. Some people who live in very warm places have never seen an orange orange.

Oranges can be eaten in many ways. Some people eat them with sugar. Others put salt on them. Lots of people eat them plain.

Some people hold an orange in their hands to eat it. Some people use a knife and fork to help them peel and eat an orange. Many people use a spoon. Some people make a small hole in one end of an orange and suck out the juice. Oranges are often squeezed to make orange juice to drink.

Not all oranges end up as food or drink. There is one country where people cut oranges in half and use them to scrub the floor!

1. This story is mainly about
    (a) orange drink.
    (b) eating fruit.
    (c) oranges.
    (d) scrubbing floors.

2. Green oranges
    (a) can't be eaten.
    (b) can be ripe.
    (c) are always bad.
    (d) are often rotten.

3. Squeezing oranges
    (a) makes juice.
    (b) makes them green.
    (c) is bad to do.
    (d) makes sugar.

4. Something that's <u>ripe</u> is
    (a) raw.
    (b) already rotten.
    (c) new.
    (d) ready to eat.

5. Some people use oranges
    (a) to scrub the floor.
    (b) instead of salt.
    (c) as clothing.
    (d) to paint the walls.

6. You can tell from this story that
    (a) people don't like oranges.
    (b) oranges need spoons.
    (c) green oranges are sour.
    (d) oranges have many uses.

Time _____ # Correct _____

Lots of people walk along Wilshire Boulevard every day. This well-known street in California is usually a nice place to walk. Lately, however, a crazy bird has been flying at people. Most birds fly the other way when they see people. But not this one. This bird dives out of the sky like an airplane at war. It pecks and scratches at people's heads. It uses its claws and its beak to hurt them.

The bird will dive and hit at just about anyone who walks by. Bald men seem to be the bird's favorites. People with lots of hair don't get hit quite as often.

Why does the bird <u>behave</u> in this very strange way? Bird experts say the bird probably is a mother with babies in a nest nearby. She probably is trying to keep her babies safe by scaring people away. When the baby birds grow up and fly away, chances are the bird will stop this odd way of acting. Then it will be safe to walk along Wilshire Boulevard once more.

1. This story takes place in
   (a) the Bronx Zoo.
   (b) California.
   (c) a large tree.
   (d) a war zone.

2. The bird dives like
   (a) a champion swimmer.
   (b) a scared rabbit.
   (c) an airplane.
   (d) a fast person.

3. People with lots of hair
   (a) are somewhat safer.
   (b) can't be hit.
   (c) will lose it.
   (d) enjoy the bird.

4. The bird dives at people
   (a) because it's fun.
   (b) to cause them harm.
   (c) to protect her babies.
   (d) to find some food.

5. Another word for <u>behave</u> is
   (a) act.
   (b) dive.
   (c) leave.
   (d) sing.

6. The bird probably will dive
   (a) until it gets tired of it.
   (b) until it gets hurt.
   (c) as long as it finds food.
   (d) as long as it has babies.

Time _____ # Correct _____

22

What could cause more than 15,000 young teenage girls to crowd into one block in New York City on a hot summer day? What could cause them to push and shove and step on each other? What could cause them to scream without stopping? Menudo, that's what.

Menudo, a Puerto Rican rock band and singing group, causes excitement like this wherever it goes. On June 15, 1983, the group was staying at the Doral Hotel in New York. Tickets for the group's concerts had all been sold out. Thousands of girls showed up at the hotel hoping to get autographs. They dreamed of going home with a scrap of paper with Menudo written on it.

The girls got no autographs, but they did get a chance to see their favorites for a minute. The five boys in Menudo waved to the girls from the safety of their hotel room on the seventh floor.

The thousands of fans screamed loudly when Menudo appeared at the window. Some of the girls fainted. Dozens were hurt as others stepped on them in an effort to get closer to the hotel. Was it worth it? "I'd go anywhere to see them," one girl said. Thousands of others would agree.

1. Menudo is a
   (a) block in New York City.
   (b) young singer.
   (c) Puerto Rican rock band.
   (d) screaming teenager.

2. The girls screamed and pushed
   (a) to hurt each other.
   (b) from extreme excitement.
   (c) for the fun of it.
   (d) to cause trouble.

3. To sign autographs is to
   (a) write one's name.
   (b) leave in a car.
   (c) spend by check.
   (d) live in a hotel.

4. Menudo stayed upstairs because
   (a) the girls all yelled.
   (b) everyone wanted them to.
   (c) it was warm outside.
   (d) it was safer there.

5. This story is mainly about
   (a) why young girls scream.
   (b) living in New York.
   (c) Menudo and its fans.
   (d) being stepped on.

6. Menudo fans are likely to
   (a) give away their tickets.
   (b) avoid large rock concerts.
   (c) wait on line quietly.
   (d) suffer to see their heroes.

Time _____ # Correct _____

Bijou is a shiny, dark bay horse who lives at Hidden Lake Farm. His name, Bijou, is the French word for jewel. His owner named him that because he was so nice-looking. Bijou likes to run and jump over fences. But most of all he likes to eat.

One summer Bijou hurt his leg and had to rest for a few weeks. Because he couldn't run around, he began to get too fat. So he was put on a <u>diet</u>. He wasn't allowed to go out and eat grass. He got three small meals a day and that was all.

Bijou was hungry and he wasn't happy. One night he tried eating all the straw in his stall. It didn't taste very good, but it was better than nothing.

The next night, Bijou got no straw, just wood chips and shavings, for his bed. They were good to sleep on but not to put in his mouth. But Bijou still found something to eat. There had been a broom near his stall. By morning, the broom was only a handle!

1. Bijou is a
    (a) hidden lake.
    (b) small jewel.
    (c) handsome horse.
    (d) type of barn.

2. A <u>diet</u> is a
    (a) kind of horse.
    (b) plan for eating.
    (c) broom.
    (d) wood chip.

3. The straw in Bijou's stall
    (a) was very green.
    (b) had too much salt in it.
    (c) came up to his knees.
    (d) didn't taste very good.

4. What did Bijou do first?
    (a) He hurt his leg.
    (b) He ate his straw.
    (c) He ate a broom.
    (d) He began to get fat.

5. This story is mainly about
    (a) Bijou and his odd meal.
    (b) how to feed a horse.
    (c) going on a diet.
    (d) a jewel of a horse.

6. You can tell from this story that
    (a) Bijou is a small horse.
    (b) Bijou eats almost anything.
    (c) some horses won't eat.
    (d) barns have two brooms.

Time _____ # Correct _____

24

Have you ever opened a Christmas present and then forgotten about it? This is a story about a present. It was opened, put aside, and then forgotten for a while. This present wasn't forgotten for long, however. An entire family is likely to remember it forever.

On Christmas Day a few years ago, a Connecticut fire fighter gave his parents a smoke alarm. They opened it and then put it back under the tree. They forgot about it as they opened other presents and then ate dinner. Everyone went to sleep that night at the usual time.

At about 2:30 in the morning, a fire broke out in the home. Many people are hurt or killed in fires, but these people were safe. The smoke alarm, the forgotten Christmas present, was still under the tree. When the fire started, the smoke alarm made a loud noise. That's what an alarm is supposed to do. The people woke up. They got out of the house in time.

Fires can sometimes happen even in houses where people are careful, although this is not likely. A smoke alarm is a good idea. Most families will never need it, but it should be there just in case. It can warn sleeping people in time for them to get out before the fire harms them.

1. This story took place
    (a) on Friday the 13th.
    (b) New Year's Day.
    (c) on the Fourth of July.
    (d) at Christmas.

2. Which happened first?
    (a) Everyone went to sleep.
    (b) The gifts were opened.
    (c) The alarm made noise.
    (d) A fire started.

3. This story is mainly about
    (a) an important Christmas gift.
    (b) noisy alarm clocks.
    (c) starting fires.
    (d) people who give gifts.

4. A smoke alarm
    (a) wakes people for breakfast.
    (b) is a silly present.
    (c) makes noise in a fire.
    (d) starts small fires.

5. The person who gave the smoke alarm to his parents
    (a) knew the danger of fire.
    (b) couldn't afford a gift.
    (c) set the fire to test it.
    (d) knew they would need it.

6. The cause of the fire was
    (a) a forgotten candle.
    (b) a winter storm.
    (c) careless people.
    (d) not told in the story.

Time _____ # Correct _____

One summer day Willie Johnson did something he should have left to Santa Claus. Willie tried to go down a chimney. Unlike Santa, however, Willie hadn't planned to leave any gifts. What he had in mind was stealing.

Willie had hoped to use the chimney to get inside a store in his neighborhood so he could rob it. He went down the chimney and ended up inside the store's <u>furnace</u>. It was summer, so the furnace was turned off. Willie couldn't open the furnace door, and he tried to climb back up the chimney again. He got stuck and couldn't go up or down.

Willie yelled for help, and two police officers came along and saved him. They cut a hole in the chimney and pulled Willie out. By this time Willie was covered with ashes and dirt from the inside of the chimney. He was glad to be out of there, but he wasn't glad very long. What do you think the police officers did next?

1. First Willie Johnson
    (a) went down the chimney.
    (b) yelled for help.
    (c) got stuck in a chimney.
    (d) was saved by police.

2. Willie wanted to
    (a) play Santa Claus.
    (b) see the furnace.
    (c) call the police.
    (d) steal from a store.

3. The furnace was off because
    (a) Willie was in the chimney.
    (b) the weather was cold.
    (c) it wasn't working well.
    (d) the weather was warm.

4. After saving Willie, the police
    (a) probably took him to jail.
    (b) gave him a nice meal.
    (c) helped him go home.
    (d) repaired the chimney.

5. A <u>furnace</u> is used to
    (a) heat a building.
    (b) store Christmas presents.
    (c) keep water cool.
    (d) do the laundry.

6. If it hadn't been summer, Willie
    (a) would have been successful.
    (b) wouldn't have screamed.
    (c) might have burned up.
    (d) could have stolen more.

Time _____ # Correct _____

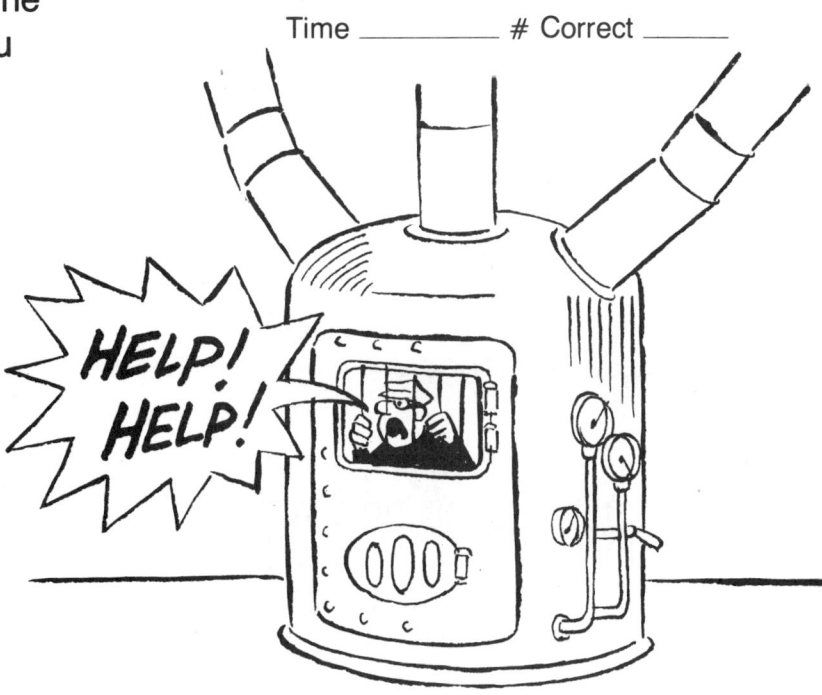

26

One day Mrs. Lopez went to take out the garbage. When she opened the garbage can, she got a big surprise. There was an alligator in it. She had never seen a real alligator before. One of her husband's shirts had a little <u>woven</u> alligator on the pocket. But that was the closest she had ever come to one.

The alligator in the can was not so small. It was more than a meter (nearly 40 inches) long. The alligator looked hungry, so Mrs. Lopez tried to find out what to feed it. She looked in a book about wild animals. The book said that alligators will eat dogs and other small animals. Then she looked at her pet dog, Rico. She decided to feed the alligator something else very quickly. She liked her dog and didn't want to lose him.

Then Mrs. Lopez called the police to come and take the animal away. She didn't want to baby-sit for an alligator any longer.

1. This story is mainly about
    (a) taking out the garbage.
    (b) feeding wild creatures.
    (c) a dog named Rico.
    (d) an alligator in a can.

2. Mrs. Lopez had a
    (a) large hungry cat.
    (b) very small garbage can.
    (c) pet dog she liked.
    (d) hungry husband.

3. The last thing Mrs. Lopez did was
    (a) feed the alligator.
    (b) hide her dog Rico.
    (c) call the police.
    (d) take out the garbage.

4. Something <u>woven</u> is
    (a) often quite hungry.
    (b) usually very dirty.
    (c) alive and kicking.
    (d) made from threads.

5. Mrs. Lopez fed the alligator to
    (a) be nice to a wild beast.
    (b) keep it from eating Rico.
    (c) show it to her husband.
    (d) make the police happy.

6. Mrs. Lopez was surprised to find the alligator because
    (a) she had just lost one.
    (b) alligators in cans are rare.
    (c) her dog had just scared it.
    (d) the police kept after them.

Time _____ # Correct _____

A swimming pool can be lots of fun. But the water in a pool can be quite dangerous, too. Brian Diaz knows that, even though he is only five years old. There's a yard with a pool in Brian's neighborhood. Often no one is home there. Brian knows to stay away. He has been told this many times, and he's a good boy who does what he should.

One day Brian went into the yard with the pool. He wasn't being naughty. He was following Andres Romero, age three, who went into the yard. "I knew it was dangerous in there," said Brian. "I thought Andres might need help." Brian was right.

Andres fell into the end of the pool where the water was very deep. He couldn't get out. He couldn't swim. He was in big trouble. Brian lay down by the edge of the pool. He grabbed Andres by the hand and pulled. "He was kind of heavy, and I almost fell in, too," Brian said. "It wasn't easy, but I held on."

The young hero pulled and pulled. He dragged Andres out of the pool. Then he put his hand on the little boy's stomach. "I pushed it down hard just like I've seen on TV," Brian explained. "Andres threw up. Lots of water came out of his mouth. I asked him if he was breathing. He said no. Then he began to cry."

1. If Brian had stayed away from the pool, as he had been told to do,
    (a) someone would have yelled.
    (b) his mother would be happy.
    (c) Andres might have drowned.
    (d) he could have been on TV.

2. The word dangerous means
    (a) all wet.
    (b) not safe.
    (c) exciting.
    (d) very bad.

3. Brian knew Andres could breathe when
    (a) Andres told him so.
    (b) the child turned blue.
    (c) the boy talked to him.
    (d) Andres couldn't talk.

4. Brian Diaz is a
    (a) good neighbor.
    (b) troubled boy.
    (c) naughty child.
    (d) poor student.

5. Which happened first?
    (a) Brian followed Andres.
    (b) Andres fell into the pool.
    (c) Andres went into the yard.
    (d) Brian took the boy's hand.

6. It would be best if Andres
    (a) never left his room.
    (b) had his own swimming pool.
    (c) stayed with an older person.
    (d) played with Brian every day.

Time _____ # Correct _____

There once was an old woman named Louisa. The only family she had was Jackie, her dog. Every day Louisa went to the bridge over the river. The dog went with her. They fished for food. Some days the fishing was good. Then they had something to eat. Some days the fishing was bad. That made the woman and the dog sad.

People liked the old woman and the dog. Sometimes people would take food to them when the fishing was bad. Then Louisa would give the people coffee to drink.

One day there was no more fishing. Trucks came to make a new road. They hurt the river and killed all the fish. No more fishing.

Soon after that, Louisa died. One of her friends put some flowers on the old fishing bridge. Jackie sat under the flowers. The little dog waited and waited. She didn't know that Louisa was never coming back to fish again.

1. Louisa was
   (a) a nice dog.
   (b) a kind of flower.
   (c) an old woman.
   (d) a bridge.

2. The old woman and the dog
   (a) fished for food.
   (b) called for help.
   (c) fished for fun.
   (d) swam in the river.

3. Because people liked Louisa and her dog, they
   (a) built a new road.
   (b) fished with them.
   (c) gave them food.
   (d) made some tea.

4. Louisa stopped fishing because
   (a) she got tired of it.
   (b) the trucks made noise.
   (c) she went away.
   (d) the fish died.

5. The word sometimes means
   (a) all the time.
   (b) never.
   (c) once in a while.
   (d) after meals.

6. Jackie waited by the bridge
   (a) to find a new owner.
   (b) because she liked flowers.
   (c) to get some fish.
   (d) hoping for Louisa's return.

Time _____ # Correct _____

Mark Schafer of New Jersey is lucky to be alive today. On December 27, 1982, Mark was driving his car along a road in Jersey City. He was driving carefully, and he wasn't doing anything wrong. His car was a Ford Pinto, which ran well enough although it wasn't very large.

Next to Mark's car a large truck—a tractor-trailer, to be exact—was going by very fast. The truck was fully loaded. It was carrying bricks, stones, and pieces of other heavy things. As the truck turned a corner, it went out of control. Somehow the truck flipped over. Everything that had been in the truck ended up on top of Mark's little car.

Mark's car was smashed. The top was pushed down almost to the seats. It didn't look much like a car anymore. People who saw the accident were sure that the driver of the car must be dead. They didn't believe that anyone could be crushed like that and still be alive. But when they finally dug Mark out, he was alive. He wasn't even badly hurt. What a lucky man! To this day, no one knows how he did it.

The truck driver wasn't hurt much either, but he had other problems. The police gave him a ticket because the truck had a bad tire in the front. That's probably what caused the accident. Then the driver got fired from his job. His boss got rid of him for going around a corner too fast.

1. Mark Schafer is lucky
   (a) he doesn't drive trucks.
   (b) because he has a job.
   (c) he's still alive.
   (d) to have so many friends.

2. The accident was
   (a) the fault of icy roads.
   (b) no one's fault.
   (c) caused by police.
   (d) the truck driver's fault.

3. An accident is something
   (a) people plan carefully.
   (b) that always hurts someone.
   (c) no one expects to happen.
   (d) the police should see.

4. After the accident,
   (a) the truck was full.
   (b) the driver got fired.
   (c) Mark drove away.
   (d) the truck went too fast.

5. People thought Mark was dead because
   (a) he had been going fast.
   (b) they saw lots of blood.
   (c) the driver told them.
   (d) his car was crushed.

6. After his accident, Mark probably
   (a) never drove anywhere again.
   (b) stayed away from trucks.
   (c) thanked the truck driver.
   (d) worked in a hospital.

Time _____ # Correct _____

30

Bugs are a very good food for small fish. Most small fish like to eat insects. The fish waits until a bug lands on top of the water. Then the fish opens its mouth and eats the bug. The archer fish has a better idea. It goes after its meals instead of waiting for them to come along.

The archer fish swims near the edge of the water. It keeps looking for food. When it sees an insect on a leaf or twig, it gets ready. It takes aim and spits at the bug. The archer fish spits drops of water. These drops of water move very fast. They go so fast that the insect is knocked into the water. Then the archer fish eats its meal.

The archer fish is a good shot. It hardly ever misses. This isn't a bad way to catch bugs. The archer fish seems to like it. However, the bugs don't like it very much at all.

1. This story is mainly about
   (a) insects that eat fish.
   (b) a fish that spits at its dinner.
   (c) how to catch the archer fish.
   (d) twigs by the side of the river.

2. The archer fish hits insects with
   (a) the fish.
   (b) a twig.
   (c) water.
   (d) air.

3. In this story, the words hardly ever mean
   (a) almost never.
   (b) ever loudly.
   (c) not very softly.
   (d) very quickly.

4. Many fish like to eat
   (a) archers.
   (b) insects.
   (c) sandwiches.
   (d) twigs.

5. The archer fish gets food by
   (a) asking nicely.
   (b) digging in the mud.
   (c) spitting at bugs.
   (d) waiting behind trees.

6. Which happens first?
   (a) The fish eats a meal.
   (b) The archer fish spits.
   (c) The fish looks for food.
   (d) The archer fish takes aim.

Time _____ # Correct _____

What makes some people live longer than others? There are some things we know, and lots of things we don't know. Eating the right foods and getting enough sleep can help keep a person healthy. People who smoke are more likely to die sooner than people who don't. But we don't really know why certain people live to be very, very old, and others do not.

Doctors had heard that many people in the Andes Mountains in South America lived to be very old. The stories said that one person had just died at the age of 168. Other people were having their 140th or 150th birthday. That's a lot of candles on a cake. Some people who heard these stories wanted to move to the Andes so they could live a long time, too.

One doctor met a woman who was 122. The next year the doctor went back and the same person was 134. Then the doctor knew what the people in the Andes Mountains did to be so old. They counted wrong, that's what!

1. The people in this story live
    (a) in the Andes Mountains.
    (b) far from any doctors.
    (c) in North America.
    (d) without any birthdays.

2. The Andes Mountains are in
    (a) South America.
    (b) North America.
    (c) Europe.
    (d) Siberia.

3. The people in this story were
    (a) not as old as it seemed.
    (b) quick to call a doctor.
    (c) ready to leave the Andes.
    (d) fairly heavy smokers.

4. One woman aged 12 years by
    (a) eating a lot.
    (b) staying up nights.
    (c) seeing the doctor.
    (d) counting wrong.

5. A healthy person is
    (a) not sick.
    (b) in need of a doctor.
    (c) often hungry.
    (d) taller than others.

6. You are likely to live longer
    (a) by moving to the Andes.
    (b) if you don't smoke.
    (c) if you eat too much.
    (d) by becoming a doctor.

Time _____ # Correct _____

32

Do you ever sneeze? Most people do sneeze from time to time. Lots of people sneeze when they are getting a cold. Some people sneeze when they breathe in things that bother them. For example, dust makes some people sneeze. Certain flowers or grasses are the reasons others sneeze. Almost anyone will sneeze if he or she gets pepper too close to the nose.

For most people, sneezing is not much of a problem. But for Andrew Watts, age 15, sneezing became a very <u>serious</u> matter.

One day, Andrew was playing hockey at school. Someone hit him under his chin with a hockey stick. It was an accident, but Andrew did get hit very hard. As soon as the hockey stick hit him, Andrew began to sneeze. He couldn't stop.

Andrew sneezed the rest of that day and all night too. He sneezed the next day and the next. He went to one doctor after another. He sneezed the entire time. No one knew what to do about a boy whose sneezing began with a hit from a hockey stick. Andrew sneezed as often as once every ten seconds.

Andrew was getting very tired of sneezing. He sneezed for 52 days. Then as suddenly as the sneezes had started, they stopped. Andrew was very happy. "I had almost forgotten what it was like to live without sneezing," he said.

1. This story is mainly about
    (a) going to the doctor.
    (b) getting hit with a stick.
    (c) Andrew and his sneezing.
    (d) playing hockey at school.

2. Sneezing is often caused by
    (a) dust or pepper.
    (b) going to the doctor.
    (c) playing hockey.
    (d) wearing a sweater.

3. When Andrew stopped sneezing,
    (a) he was very unhappy.
    (b) everyone laughed at him.
    (c) doctors made him cry.
    (d) he was quite happy.

4. Which happened first? Andrew
    (a) began to sneeze.
    (b) stopped sneezing.
    (c) went to doctors.
    (d) was hit by a stick.

5. Something <u>serious</u> is
    (a) caused by a sneeze.
    (b) nothing to laugh at.
    (c) done on a field.
    (d) found in the sky.

6. Doctors couldn't help Andrew because
    (a) they didn't try hard.
    (b) he wouldn't let them.
    (c) his case was so unusual.
    (d) sneezing lasts forever.

Time _____ # Correct _____

For many years, postal workers have been delivering the mail in all kinds of weather. The mail is delivered in rain or snow. It's delivered on very hot days and on days when everything is icy cold.

Although bad weather doesn't stop the postal workers from doing their job, there is one thing that can stop them. That one thing is a dog.

The country's head postal worker has given a warning to people who own dogs. "If your dog bites, you may get no mail." There's a good reason for this warning. In the last year, about 5,700 postal workers were bitten by dogs.

The post office may refuse to deliver mail to a house with a loose dog that bites. If the dog is really wild and runs loose off the owner's land, then the worker may <u>avoid</u> going to that block at all. If this happens, then everyone in the neighborhood would have to go to the post office to pick up the mail.

1. This story is mainly about
    (a) working in bad weather.
    (b) lazy postal workers.
    (c) how to do a job.
    (d) dogs and mail delivery.

2. Rain and snow
    (a) make the dogs bite.
    (b) are very pleasant.
    (c) don't stop the mail.
    (d) wash off the address.

3. If your dog bites,
    (a) you may get no mail.
    (b) you'll need two dogs.
    (c) no one will visit you.
    (d) you should bite back.

4. To <u>avoid</u> means to
    (a) deliver something.
    (b) have a good time.
    (c) empty something.
    (d) stay away from.

5. In one year, dogs bit
    (a) all their neighbors.
    (b) 570 delivery people.
    (c) 5,700 postal workers.
    (d) most neighborhood cats.

6. The owner of a biting dog
    (a) should do without mail.
    (b) might buy two more.
    (c) could tie the dog up.
    (d) should feed it more.

Time _____ # Correct _____

34

June Soper lives in a teepee in Michigan. She is part Cherokee Indian. Like many of her Native American ancestors before her, Ms. Soper calls the teepee her home.

The teepee has waterproof cloth walls to keep out snow and rain. Straw and pine branches help keep out the cold. Layers of earth, pine needles, and fur rugs keep the floor warm. Ms. Soper built her teepee herself. She had built ten others that people used for special powwows. This was the first teepee she built that someone could live in.

In some ways, life in June Soper's teepee is like teepee life long ago. She gets heat from a fire. Visitors to the teepee sit on the floor with their legs crossed. There are no chairs.

In some other ways, Ms. Soper's teepee is very different from other teepees. She gets extra heat from an electric heater. She pays rent every month for use of the land. Her teepee has a television set and a telephone.

Ms. Soper is well known in her area. Lots of people know her and like her. Sometimes disk jockeys call her and ask her how she is doing. In bad weather, they call to find out if she is all right. Then they tell the people listening to the radio that their friend, June Soper, is doing fine.

1. June Soper lives in a
    (a) radio station.
    (b) powwow.
    (c) teepee.
    (d) pine tree.

2. Ms. Soper gets heat from
    (a) a fire and a heater.
    (b) the sun and the moon.
    (c) calling her friends.
    (d) an oil burner.

3. Visitors to the teepee
    (a) sit on chairs.
    (b) watch movies.
    (c) sit on the floor.
    (d) argue a lot.

4. Chances are, Ms. Soper lives in a teepee because she
    (a) can't afford anything else.
    (b) needs it for her powwows.
    (c) likes the life of her ancestors.
    (d) isn't smart enough to move.

5. You can tell that Ms. Soper
    (a) dislikes any new things.
    (b) is glad to be Native American.
    (c) enjoys being cold and wet.
    (d) is hard to get along with.

6. People call Ms. Soper because
    (a) they think she is poor.
    (b) there is no one else.
    (c) she serves good dinners.
    (d) they care about her.

Time _____ # Correct _____

To see a live fish, where would you look? Would you look in a lake or a stream? Would you look in the sea or a river? Would you look in a glass fish tank in someone's house? What all these places have in common is that they have water in them.

Most people would never think of looking on the ground or up a tree for a fish. But there's a kind of fish that might be found out of water. This fish is called the mudskipper. Its name comes from the way it uses its tail to move along mud flats. It can skip faster than a person trying to catch it.

The mudskipper is an odd sort of fish. Not only can it move along on mud, but it can climb trees. The front fins of the mudskipper are like arms, and it can use them to pull itself part-way up a tree. This fish climbs trees to catch insects for food.

The mudskipper is a very strange fish indeed. It seems to spend almost as much time out of the water as in it.

1. Most live fish are
    (a) on tree branches.
    (b) in the mud.
    (c) in fish stores.
    (d) in the water.

2. A mudskipper can
    (a) jump high.
    (b) sing and skip.
    (c) climb trees.
    (d) fly like a bird.

3. This story is mainly about
    (a) climbing trees.
    (b) fish that swim.
    (c) skipping in the mud.
    (d) an unusual fish.

4. It is NOT true that
    (a) some fish climb trees.
    (b) mudskippers eat bugs.
    (c) mudskippers must be dry.
    (d) fins never move.

5. The mudskipper is named for
    (a) the way it eats mud.
    (b) eating muddy insects.
    (c) climbing up trees.
    (d) the way it moves.

6. A mudskipper's front fins are
    (a) like arms.
    (b) really legs.
    (c) small tails.
    (d) jump ropes.

Time _____ # Correct _____

Beaverdale, Pennsylvania, is a town which has had bad luck over the years. In January, 1976, this tiny mining town burned down. The fire wiped out 13 of the 15 buildings in the main part of town. The loss was more than a million dollars.

This was not the first time that the town had burned. In 1911, there was a fire that burned down all the buildings on the town's main street. People built the town up again. In 1932, another fire hit the main street. Again the town was rebuilt.

The 1976 fire was very hard to fight. It was a windy day which was very cold. The water froze, and fire fighters couldn't pour water on the fire. There wasn't much to do except watch things burn. Three families lost their homes. Many stores lost everything. But before the fire was over, people were already talking about rebuilding. The people of Beaverdale care about their town.

1. Beaverdale is a
    (a) very small mining town.
    (b) city in Pennsylvania.
    (c) place to keep animals.
    (d) forest fire.

2. Beaverdale has burned down
    (a) once since 1911.
    (b) at least ten times.
    (c) three times.
    (d) twice in a year.

3. The 1976 fire was hard to fight because
    (a) no one would help.
    (b) the water was frozen.
    (c) the fire was hot.
    (d) people didn't care.

4. Rebuilding means
    (a) setting a fire.
    (b) making again.
    (c) selling things.
    (d) driving a truck.

5. Which happened last? The people
    (a) lost their homes.
    (b) watched things burn.
    (c) saw fire start.
    (d) talked about rebuilding.

6. You can tell the people care because they
    (a) move around a lot.
    (b) set large fires.
    (c) help the fire fighters.
    (d) want to rebuild the town.

Time _____ # Correct _____

Barney Clark's heart didn't work very well. The heart pumps blood to all the other parts of the body. A person whose heart doesn't work soon dies.

Barney was a brave man. He didn't want to die, so he let the doctors try something new. Barney's own heart was damaged. It was too badly hurt to be repaired. Doctors knew they couldn't make Barney's own heart better so they gave him a new one on December 2, 1982. It was Barney's only chance.

Barney's new heart was made of plastic. It was the first time doctors had ever tried anything like this. Experiments had been done with plastic hearts for animals, but Barney was the first human to get one.

People all over the world sent best wishes to Barney Clark. They all hoped he would get better. Every day the newspapers had a story about how he was doing. At Christmas time, Barney was still very sick. But without his plastic heart he probably wouldn't have lived even that long. Many people sent Christmas cards to Barney and his wife, who visited him every day in the hospital.

Barney Clark never got completely better. His plastic heart worked well, but the rest of his body was very tired. He died on March 23, 1983. What doctors learned from Barney Clark may save many lives some day. The man's courage set an example for everyone.

1. This story is mainly about
    (a) Barney Clark's wife.
    (b) doctors and what they do.
    (c) going to the hospital.
    (d) a very brave man.

2. Without a new heart, Barney
    (a) would have died sooner.
    (b) would have gotten better.
    (c) would have been rich.
    (d) would be here.

3. Because Barney was brave,
    (a) he couldn't see a doctor.
    (b) his wife was younger.
    (c) he dared to be first.
    (d) he loved his animals.

4. First, Barney Clark
    (a) got a plastic heart.
    (b) became very sick.
    (c) got cards from people.
    (d) died on March 23.

5. Something that's damaged is
    (a) very expensive.
    (b) hurt or injured.
    (c) strong.
    (d) nice to look at.

6. People sent Barney cards
    (a) to ask him for money.
    (b) to find out his age.
    (c) because they cared.
    (d) to feel better themselves.

Time _____ # Correct _____

Paul Chan is a painter, but not many painters work the way he does. He does not paint houses, inside or outside. He does not paint little pictures. What does he do? How is his work different from that of other painters?

Paul Chan lives and works in New York City. He paints high above New York's famous Times Square. On what does he paint? He paints on the <u>enormous</u> signs that tower over the people in New York's theater district.

Mr. Chan's works of art are certainly not small. One recent creation stood 35 feet high. It was more than one city block long. It was so huge that the artist had to paint it in many smaller sections. Each part was four feet by eight feet in size.

Mr. Chan's work is so large it has been called bigger than life. Are you still having a hard time understanding how large his work really is? Perhaps this fact will help you. Mr. Chan once did a picture of Sidney Poitier, the well-known actor. On the completed sign, the eye of Mr. Poitier was five feet seven inches high. Mr. Chan is exactly five feet seven inches tall.

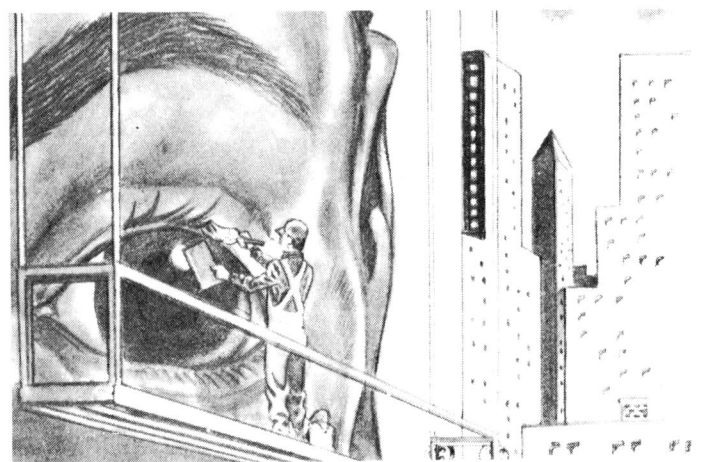

1. Paul Chan's job is to
    (a) go to the theater.
    (b) paint huge signs.
    (c) paint tall buildings.
    (d) police Times Square.

2. This story is mainly about
    (a) Sidney Poitier, an actor.
    (b) going to New York.
    (c) painting little pictures.
    (d) Paul Chan's huge art.

3. The word <u>enormous</u> means
    (a) like an animal.
    (b) smaller than some.
    (c) very large or huge.
    (d) in the eyes.

4. From a Times Square sidewalk, you could see Chan's work by
    (a) taking a bus.
    (b) looking up.
    (c) buying a map.
    (d) asking the police.

5. On one of Chan's signs, there is
    (a) an eye as tall as he is.
    (b) a man painted blue.
    (c) eyes partly closed.
    (d) an eye that winks.

6. Mr. Chan once painted
    (a) all of Times Square.
    (b) New York's mayor.
    (c) an actress.
    (d) Sidney Poitier.

Time _____ # Correct _____

Ice hockey is a rough sport. Some people feel that girls should not play hockey on a boys' team. Michele Emerson, a young woman from Waukegan, Illinois, would not agree with those people. She has good reason.

Several years ago, when Michele was ten, she was a hockey player on a boys' team. She was a very good player, and the team's only goalie. Her team needed her. A good goalie is necessary to keep the other team from scoring. It's tough to win a game without a good player guarding the goal.

Ms. Emerson's team went to Canada for an important game. Both teams wanted to win, because the game was for the North American Silver Stick Championship. But Michele was not allowed to play, because there was a firm rule that only boys could play in the Silver Stick matches. So, Michele, her team's only goalie, had to sit out the game on the bench.

Michele didn't make a big fuss. She let her team play without her, because if she had tried to play the team would have been sent home. "It's a dumb rule," she said at the time. "But I didn't want to hurt the rest of the team and make them lose the game because of me."

Without Michele, the team had to use six skaters instead of five skaters and a goalkeeper. The final score was 6 to 4. They lost.

1. Michele Emerson's sport was
   (a) basketball.
   (b) field hockey.
   (c) ice hockey.
   (d) figure skating.

2. The hockey teams in this story
   (a) used six players.
   (b) had five goalkeepers.
   (c) were all girls.
   (d) used silver sticks.

3. A firm rule is one that
   (a) melts with the ice.
   (b) favors little girls.
   (c) can't be changed.
   (d) is easy to break.

4. Michele probably played hockey
   (a) to prove a point.
   (b) so she would fail in school.
   (c) because she enjoyed it.
   (d) to meet lots of boys.

5. Michele didn't play in Canada because
   (a) she didn't want to.
   (b) goalies weren't welcome.
   (c) she fell and got hurt.
   (d) they wouldn't let her.

6. It's likely that Michele's team lost because
   (a) the team wasn't any good.
   (b) they didn't try hard enough.
   (c) they didn't have a goalie.
   (d) Michele wanted them to lose.

Time _____ # Correct _____

40

Ron Bricker worked in a steel mill until he got laid off. It looked as if he would never get his old job back. Steel companies in the United States weren't doing as much business as they used to do. People weren't buying as many American cars, so less steel was being used. <u>Times were tough.</u>

Mr. Bricker decided to try another trade. So, in 1983 he went to computer school. One day President Reagan visited the school. Mr. Bricker asked the President to help him get a new job. The President did. Mr. Bricker got a job fixing computers. He went on television and told everyone how the President had helped him.

There was one big problem. Mr. Bricker didn't really like his new job. It was better than nothing, but he wasn't happy. The new job paid only half as much as Mr. Bricker had made working in the steel mill. Every day he wished for his old job back. Then he quit the job the President had helped him get. Working with computers just wasn't for him. He planned to get a job driving a truck. But he didn't need to. Things were getting better. The steel mill called. They needed Ron Bricker again.

1. This story is mainly about
    (a) driving a truck.
    (b) working with computers.
    (c) Ronald Reagan.
    (d) a man and his job.

2. The President helped Mr. Bricker
    (a) get more money.
    (b) study about computers.
    (c) return to the steel mill.
    (d) get a new job.

3. When times are tough,
    (a) things are hard to chew.
    (b) people have three jobs.
    (c) life can be difficult.
    (d) everyone has fun.

4. Mr. Bricker quit his job because
    (a) he found three new ones.
    (b) the President called him.
    (c) it wasn't right for him.
    (d) his wife had money.

5. When the steel mill called,
    (a) Mr. Bricker didn't answer.
    (b) the computers blew up.
    (c) Mr. Bricker was happy.
    (d) the President laughed.

6. What happened first? Mr. Bricker
    (a) got his job back.
    (b) went to computer school.
    (c) quit his computer job.
    (d) got laid off.

Time _____ # Correct _____

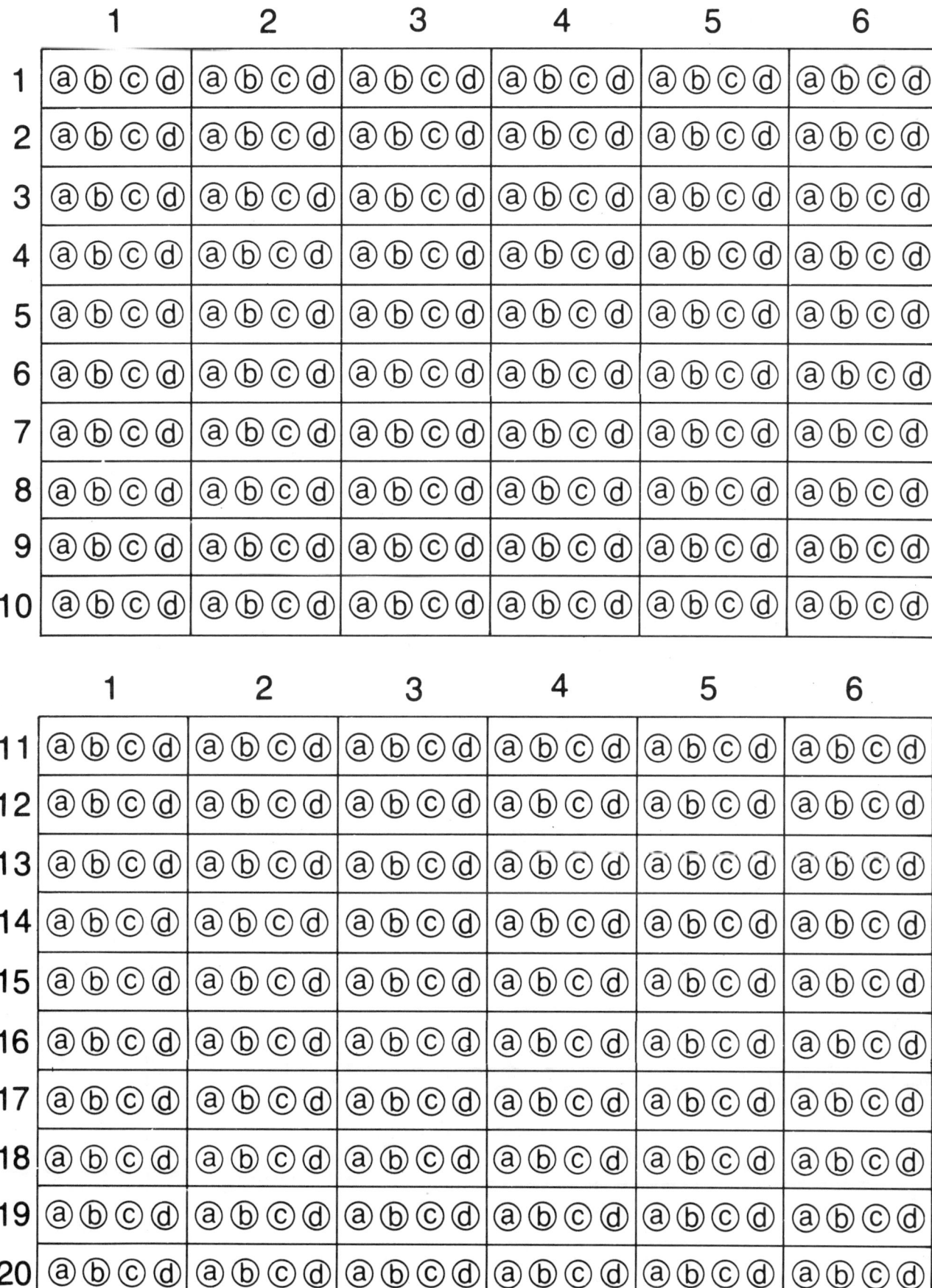

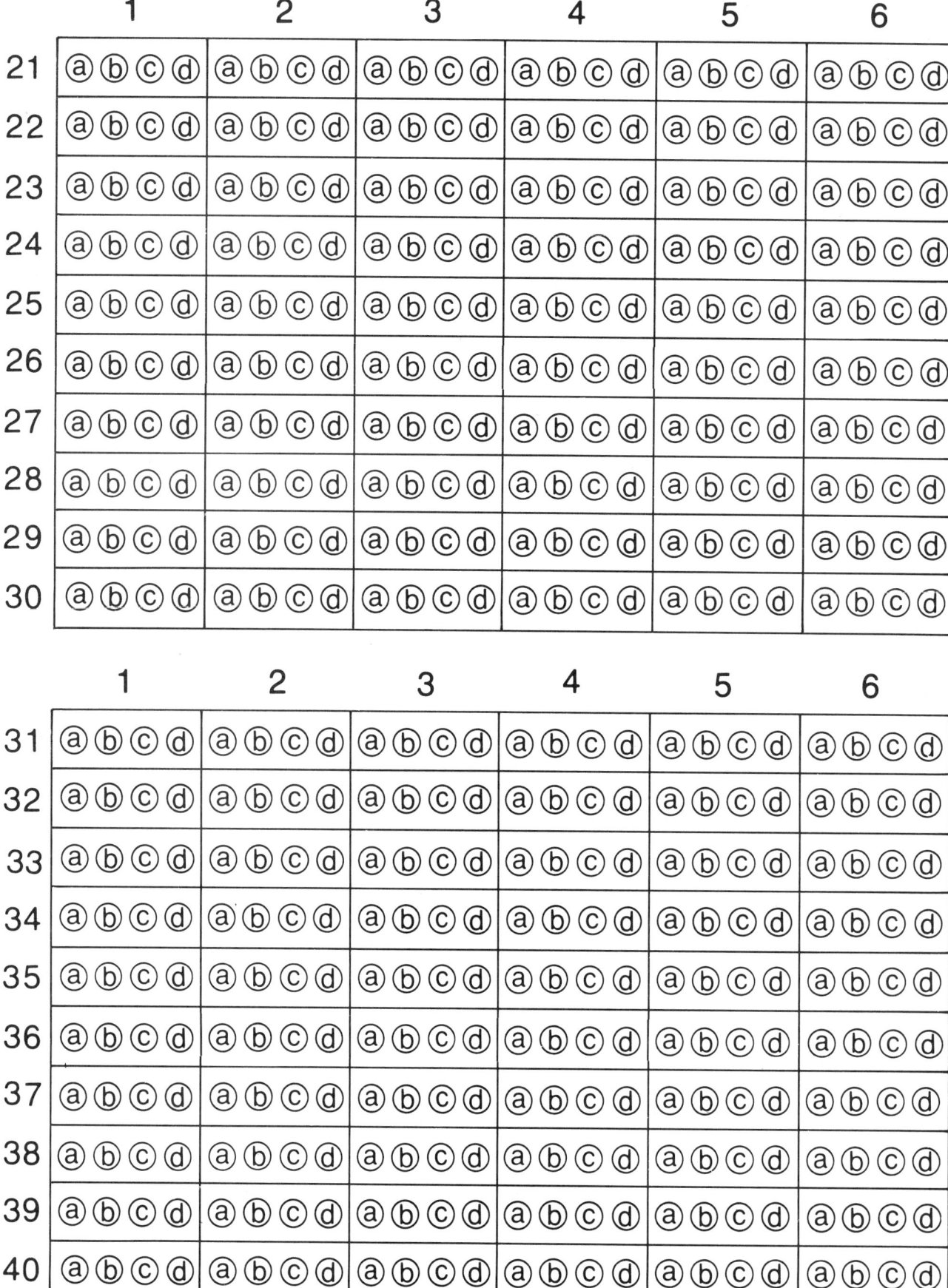

Answer Key

	1	2	3	4	5	6
1	b	b	d	a	c	b
2	c	b	d	d	b	b
3	d	b	b	a	c	d
4	b	d	c	c	a	b
5	c	c	c	c	b	b
6	a	d	c	c	b	d
7	b	d	c	b	c	b
8	d	c	b	c	a	a
9	a	b	b	b	d	d
10	b	c	a	a	b	d

	1	2	3	4	5	6
11	a	c	d	c	d	b
12	b	b	c	a	d	b
13	a	d	b	c	b	d
14	b	d	c	d	b	a
15	b	d	b	c	d	b
16	b	d	d	c	a	b
17	d	d	c	b	d	c
18	c	c	b	b	d	b
19	c	c	d	b	a	c
20	c	b	a	d	a	d

Answer Key

	1	2	3	4	5	6
21	ⓑ	ⓒ	ⓐ	ⓒ	ⓐ	ⓓ
22	ⓒ	ⓑ	ⓐ	ⓓ	ⓒ	ⓓ
23	ⓒ	ⓑ	ⓓ	ⓐ	ⓐ	ⓑ
24	ⓓ	ⓑ	ⓐ	ⓒ	ⓐ	ⓓ
25	ⓐ	ⓓ	ⓓ	ⓐ	ⓐ	ⓒ
26	ⓓ	ⓒ	ⓒ	ⓓ	ⓑ	ⓑ
27	ⓒ	ⓑ	ⓒ	ⓐ	ⓒ	ⓒ
28	ⓒ	ⓐ	ⓒ	ⓓ	ⓒ	ⓓ
29	ⓒ	ⓓ	ⓒ	ⓑ	ⓓ	ⓑ
30	ⓑ	ⓒ	ⓐ	ⓑ	ⓒ	ⓒ

	1	2	3	4	5	6
31	ⓐ	ⓐ	ⓐ	ⓓ	ⓐ	ⓑ
32	ⓒ	ⓐ	ⓓ	ⓓ	ⓑ	ⓒ
33	ⓓ	ⓒ	ⓐ	ⓓ	ⓒ	ⓒ
34	ⓒ	ⓐ	ⓒ	ⓒ	ⓑ	ⓓ
35	ⓓ	ⓒ	ⓓ	ⓒ	ⓓ	ⓐ
36	ⓐ	ⓒ	ⓑ	ⓑ	ⓓ	ⓓ
37	ⓓ	ⓐ	ⓒ	ⓑ	ⓑ	ⓒ
38	ⓑ	ⓓ	ⓒ	ⓑ	ⓐ	ⓓ
39	ⓒ	ⓐ	ⓒ	ⓒ	ⓓ	ⓒ
40	ⓓ	ⓓ	ⓒ	ⓒ	ⓒ	ⓓ

Progress Plotter

Skills Tracker

	1	2	3	4	5	6	7	8	9	10
Details	4	1, 2	1, 3, 4	1, 3	2, 3, 4	4	2	2	2, 3, 4	1, 3
Sequence	4	—	1	—	5	6	4	—	—	4
Context	2	4	2	5	6	3	—	3	5, 6	6
Main Idea	1	—	—	2	1	1	1	1	1	—
Inference	3, 5, 6	3, 6	6	6	—	2, 5	3, 5, 6	4, 5	—	5
Cause & Effect	3	2	5	1, 4	—	5	3, 5	4	—	5
Pred. Outcomes	6	5	—	6	—	6	4, 6	—	—	4
Underst. Char.	6	5, 6	3, 4, 6	6	—	2	2, 5	5, 6	3	2, 5

	11	12	13	14	15	16	17	18	19	20
Details	3	1, 2, 6	—	1, 5, 6	4	1, 5	1	2, 3	2	2, 3, 5
Sequence	—	—	5	2, 6	5	2	—	—	6	—
Context	4	3, 5	3	3	3, 6	4	2, 5	4	—	4
Main Idea	1	—	1	—	1	3	—	1	3	1
Inference	2, 5, 6	4	2, 4, 6	4	2	6	3, 4, 6	6	1, 3, 5	6
Cause & Effect	2, 6	4, 6	2	4	4	5	—	3, 5	2	3
Pred. Outcomes	2	—	5, 6	2	—	6	4	6	—	—
Underst. Char.	5, 6	1, 2, 4	2, 6	1	4	1, 2, 5, 6	—	6	1, 3, 5	—

	21	22	22	24	25	26	27	28	29	30
Detail	1, 2	1	1, 3	1	2, 3	2, 3	—	1, 2, 3	4	2, 4
Sequence	—	—	4	2	1	3	5	—	4	6
Context	5	3	2	4	5	4	2	5	3	3
Main Idea	—	5	5	3	—	1	—	—	—	1
Inference	3, 4	4, 6	6	3, 5	4, 6	5, 6	1, 6	4, 6	1, 2, 5, 6	5
Cause & Effect	4	2, 4	—	6	3	5, 6	1, 3	3, 4, 6	1, 2, 5	5
Pred. Outcomes	6	6	4	2, 5	4, 6	—	1	6	6	6
Underst. Char.	4, 6	2, 4, 6	1, 6	5	2	5, 6	1, 3, 4	3, 4, 6	1	5

	31	32	33	34	35	36	37	38	39	40
Detail	1, 2	2, 3	2, 5	1, 2, 3	2, 5, 6	1, 2	—	1, 6	1, 2	2
Sequence	—	4	—	—	—	5	4	—	—	6
Context	5	5	4	—	—	4	5	3	3	3
Main Idea	3	1	1	—	3	—	1	2	—	1
Inference	3, 4, 6	6	3, 6	4, 5, 6	1, 4	6	2	4, 5	4, 5, 6	3, 4
Cause & Effect	4	2, 3	3	2, 4, 6	5	3	2, 3	—	5, 6	3, 4, 5
Pred. Outcomes	6	4	3	—	—	5	2	4	—	6
Underst. Char.	3	3, 6	3, 6	4, 5, 6	2, 5, 6	6	3, 6	2	4, 5	4, 5